THE TRIUMPHAL ENTRY OF CHRIST

AT THE FIFTH DARK NEW MOON OF 2022 - THE TRUE DAY OF PENTECOST!

By Christine Cooper
Copyright 2022 All rights reserved
All scripture quoted is taken from the King James Version

This is the fourth book to a series:

The Transformed Christians (1)

The Making of an Overcomer in Christ (2)

A Dark Moon Rapture! (3)

CONTENTS:

Introduction   5

CHAPTER 1 : *The Four Key Events*   9

CHAPTER 2 : *The Four Key Events in Linear Time*   21

CHAPTER 3 : *The Four Key Events in 2022*   31

INTRODUCTION

While we understand biblical accounts to be happening in a linear chronological order, the account of Christ's work in the gospels seem to be also happening in a 'cycle or circle' manner, in that the end of a matter is seen at the beginning, as seen in how Jesus was able to heal the sick *even before* He became the atonement for our healing (see Matthew 8:17). It is this great mystery of timing in the gospels that truly shows how Jesus Christ is indeed the Alpha and the Omega - the beginning and the end, yet also without beginning and without ending, after the order of Melchizedek - *'Without father, without mother, without descent, having neither beginning of days, nor end of life; but made like unto the Son of God; abideth a priest continually.' (Hebrews 7:3).* Therefore, when we read the gospel accounts in regards to the ministry of Jesus Christ, in order for us to see God's amazing spiritual time, we must consider how time is both linear (which is how we understand time, things happen *after* each other), but it is also circular (spiritual - outside of linear time, that the end happens at the beginning) which means time can in a way wrap itself around itself to bring the end of a matter to happen at the beginning, and even before the beginning (the first event) has even happened! This means that an event can happen before the proceeding one has come, but yet the proceeding event one has *already come* and happened. Yes, this confusion you may be feeling in your mind right now is evident of how our natural minds are limited in grasping the spiritual dimensions of God's time. But don't let your natural mind limit your understanding, because remember as born-again Christians you are spiritual, so you can understand spiritual things of God because the Spirit of God makes it known to you, therefore allow Him to show you spiritual truths, as it says- *'But God hath revealed them unto us by his Spirit: for the Spirit searcheth all things, yea, the deep things of God.' 1 Corinthians 1:10.*

The spiritual understanding of time (circular, outside of linear time) is vitally important as it helps us to understand four key events of Christ, notably the triumphal entry, which while we read in scripture happens before Passover, it is actually the end of a matter manifested at the beginning - meaning, the Passion of the Christ has already taken place, even though the triumphal entry happens before the Passion of the Christ has even begun! This spiritual 'circle of time' helps us understand how Jesus was able to ride into Jerusalem on a donkey, as what was prophesied in *Zechariah 9:9 'Rejoice greatly, O daughter of Zion; shout, O daughter of Jerusalem: behold, thy King cometh unto thee: he is just, and having salvation; lowly, and riding upon an ass, and upon a colt the foal of an ass.'* was already fulfilled by Jesus Christ even before He went through His passion, but yet it was also *after* having gone through His passion to be the perfect atonement and establish a new covenant, in order to be the victorious coming King, having already conquered death, sin, and the devil.

This great mystery of the triumphal entry showing the victorious work of Christ even before His passion yet also being after His passion, is seen when we look in the scripture that reveals a 'three-day difference' to the triumphal entry of Christ, which happens in the gospel of John on the '9th day' and the other three synoptic gospels was on the 13th day (the day before the Passover), which is three days difference between them. This 'three-day difference' of His triumphal entry (10th, 11th and 12th days), shows a mystery of circular spiritual time that shows we have already gone through the Passion of the Christ because of the prophetic 'Sign of Jonah' (a three-day time period difference) that takes place between the 'two' triumphal entry days (obviously only one, but the three-day difference of it's timing shows two) shows a circle of time that the triumphal entry happens *after* the sign of Jonah but *also even before* Jesus went through His Passion, to show He has *already gone through* His passion!

So in order for this mystery to be seen we need to take into account an event that happened before the triumphal entry- when Jesus was anointed. Then we will look at the other key events, such as the Cleansing of the Temple and the Cursing of the Fig tree. Hence, there are four key events: The Anointing of Jesus (J.A), Triumphal Entry (T.E), Cursing of the Fig Tree (C.F) and the Cleansing of the Temple (C.T). Please note that the cursing of the fig tree event happens after the cleansing of the temple, but yet we will discuss it before, to show how the Cleansing of the Temple (fourth and last key event) brings it all back to the beginning, hence back to the triumphal entry of Christ.

The importance of knowing all these spiritual times of these four key events that go on in the gospel scriptures is because they are relevant for our day today, as they show us when the day of Christ's visitation (His triumphal entry) is going to happen, which is between 30th April - 1st May 2022, the fifth dark new moon of 2022. Therefore, when Christ appears, Christians will suddenly be transformed by receiving the redemption of their bodies, *before* the Feast of Passover on the Hebrew lunar calendar (*The Overcomer Calendar*) but *after* the finished work of Christ!

CHAPTER 1

THE FOUR KEY EVENTS

The four key events:

    1) JESUS ANOINTED (J.A)

    2) TRIUMPHAL ENTRY (T.E)

    3) JESUS CURSES THE FIG TREE (C.F)

    4) JESUS CLEANSES THE TEMPLE (C.T)

(SEE FOUR CHARTS ON FOLLOWING PAGES)

THE MYSTERY OF 3 DAYS DIFFERENCE IN THE GOSPELS

THE ANOINTING OF JESUS

1	2	3	4	5	6	7
8	9	10	11	12	13	14 PASSOVER

GOSPEL OF JOHN (SIX DAYS BEFORE PASSOVER JOHN 12:1)

SYNOPTIC GOSPELS (TWO DAYS BEFORE PASSOVER MATT 26:1 & MARK 14:1)

THE MYSTERY OF 3 DAYS DIFFERENCE IN THE GOSPELS

THE TRIUMPHAL ENTRY

1	2	3	4	5	6	7
8	9	10	11	12	13	14 PASSOVER

■ GOSPEL OF JOHN (THE 'NEXT DAY' AFTER ANOINTING OF JESUS - JOHN 12:12)

■ SYNOPTIC GOSPELS (NO TIME PERIOD STATED MATT 21, MK 11, LK 19)

THE MYSTERY OF 3 DAYS DIFFERENCE IN THE GOSPELS

THE CURSING OF THE FIG TREE

1	2	3	4	5	6	7
8	9	10	11	12	13	14 PASSOVER

■ GOSPEL OF JOHN (NO MENTION OF FIG TREE BEING CURSED)

■ SYNOPTIC GOSPELS (NO TIME PERIOD STATED BUT IT FOLLOWS THE TRI. ENTRY)

THE MYSTERY OF 3 DAYS DIFFERENCE IN THE GOSPELS

CLEANSING OF THE TEMPLE

1	2	3	4	5	6	7
8	9	10	11	12	13	14 PASSOVER

■ GOSPEL OF JOHN ………… WE WILL COME BACK TO THIS! :)
■ SYNOPTIC GOSPELS (NO TIME PERIOD STATED BUT IT FOLLOWS THE TRI. ENTRY)

The first key event, the Anointing of Jesus, begins the four key events which all happen in the week prior to the Feast of Passover, and reveal a three-day difference between the gospel of John and the three synoptic gospels (Matthew, Mark and Luke). In the gospel of John 12:1, Mary anointed Jesus' feet '*six* days before Passover', which would be the 8th day of the first month (as Passover is on the 14th day); and yet in the two gospels of Matthew 26:1 and Mark 14:1 it was only '*two* days before Passover', when Mary anointed Jesus' head, hence the 12th day of the first month. It is through these initial scriptures of the first of four key events when Jesus is anointed (J.A), that we can clearly see a 'three day difference' within the gospels. Hence, Jesus was anointed on His feet on the '8th day' in the gospel of John, and yet He was anointed on His head on the '12th day' in the gospels of Matthew and Mark, thus there is a three-day difference between them - the 9th to 11th days.

It is worth also mentioning here in regards to the anointing of Jesus that there is also a difference of where Mary anoints Him between the gospels, in that Mary anoints Jesus' *'feet'* in the gospel of John and yet it's His *'head'* in the gospels of Matthew and Mark, in which both areas (His feet and His head) are also separated by these three days difference of timing. Therefore, could these differences of areas (body parts - the feet and the head) that are anointed represent the beginning (head) and the end (feet) of a matter? Could it also represent Christ as the Head and His feet as the Body of Christ? Could it represent that the 'head' is anointed for a King and the 'feet' is anointed for a High Priest, or is it the other way around? It is worth considering these differences of areas of the head and feet that are anointed in your own heart, but for now, this book will focus on the circle of time of how these four key events show a 'three day difference'; and how the three synoptic gospels 'jump ahead a day' when Jesus goes through His Passion (it was Passover Night on the night of His betrayal in the three synoptic gospels but it was before Passover on the night of His betrayal in the gospel of John, see John 13:1).

The Triumphal Entry is the second key event during the mysterious three-day difference in the four gospels of Jesus Christ. It follows the first key event (The Anointing of Jesus), as it happens the following day after the evening meal that Jesus had with Mary, Martha and Lazarus. This is stated in the gospel of John ch. 12: 12-15 *'On the next day much people that were come to the feast, when they heard that Jesus was coming to Jerusalem, Took branches of palm trees, and went forth to meet him, and cried, Hosanna: Blessed is the King of Israel that cometh in the name of the Lord. And Jesus, when he had found a young ass, sat thereon; as it is written, Fear not, daughter of Sion: behold, thy King cometh, sitting on an ass's colt.'* (This was written in Zechariah 9:9). Hence, in the gospel of John we can see that the Triumphal Entry (T.E) happens the next day after Jesus was anointed. However, in the three synoptic gospels there is no mention of when the triumphal entry happens only that it is written in the three synoptic gospels of Matthew ch.21, Mark ch.11 and Luke ch.19 which is *before* the anointing of Jesus (exception to Luke's gospel). Therefore the second key event 'The Triumphal Entry' (T.E) being written in scripture in the gospels of Matthew and Mark before the anointing of Jesus could show us another confirmation that there is a cycle of events rather than a linear flow of these four key events. This shows us why the scriptural flow of the Triumphal Entry happening before the Feast of Passover, is actually after Jesus made atonement through His own body as being the Passover Lamb of God. Hence, He was able to ride into Jerusalem as King and High Priest on the day of His visitation prior to His Passion yet after having already accomplished it! So what the 'cycle' of these key events show us is that they begin and end before Passover happens, and because there is a three-day difference between them for a prophetic 'Sign of Jonah', it also shows that that the Passover has already happened, which is why Jesus was able to say to the thief on the cross *'today'* he would be with Him in paradise (see Luke 23:43), and why He didn't say 'in three days and three nights time', because the 'Sign of Jonah' (three-day difference) had already happened beforehand.

However, in order to keep things as simple as possible in this book, the four key events will be shown in a linear flow for all four gospels, then once that is seen, it should be possible to grasp the 'cycle' of these four key events for you to be able to understand and see how they end before they even happen. Therefore, in keeping to the linear flow, the triumphal entry of Christ in the three synoptic gospels is timed to happen the next day after the anointing of Jesus. Hence because He was anointed on the 12th day (two days before Passover, Matthew 26:1 & Mark 14:1), the triumphal entry will be the next day, as revealed by the gospel of John that the triumphal entry happened the next day after the anointing of Jesus, hence in the three synoptic gospels that would be the 13th day of the first month.

The third key event is the Cursing of the Fig Tree (C.F), and it is not mentioned in either of the gospels of Luke and John, but it is mentioned in the two remaining gospels Matthew and Mark (see Matthew 21:1-20 & Mark 11:1-14), which happens after the triumphal entry. There is a significant difference between the cursing of the fig tree in the gospel of Matthew and the gospel of Mark, in terms of when it withers, which simply put is that when Jesus cursed it, it withers *'at once'* in the gospel of Matthew 21: 18-22 but it withers *'the next day'* in the gospel of Mark 11:12-25; and it's this mystery of the timing of the day difference of the fig tree withering (and also after when Jesus cleanses the temple in Mark) which shows how the day advances ahead in the three synoptic gospels in comparison to the gospel of John for the Passion of the Christ, which is clearly seen from the night of His betrayal (as already mentioned).

The fourth key event is the Cleansing of the Temple (C.T) and this takes place in all four gospels and it follows the Triumphal Entry (T.E). In the gospel of John it is written about very early on in the gospel of John (in the second chapter), but in the other gospels it's towards the end of their chapters, right before the Passion of the Christ begins. This difference of where the triumphal entry and the cleansing of the temple is written in the gospels (at the beginning of the gospel of John and yet at the end of the three synoptic gospels) could also show another confirmation of why there is a 'three day difference' between them and the gospel of John, in order to show a 'cycle' of events to have a prophetic 'Sign of Jonah' before His Passion, rather than it just being a 'linear' flow.

So in summary, the triumphal entry comes after the anointing of Jesus feet, followed by the cleansing of the temple which happens on the same day as the triumphal entry, and yet in the gospel of Mark, the cleansing of the temple and the cursing of the fig tree happen the day after the triumphal entry, which shows us how the three synoptic gospels move ahead a day from the gospel of John, for the timing of the

Passion of the Christ, which begins with the night of His betrayal. Here is a summary chart to help you see the flow of these four key events:

THE MYSTERY OF 3 DAYS DIFFERENCE IN THE GOSPELS

GOSPELS FLOW OF KEY EVENTS

1) JESUS ANOINTED (J.A)
2) TRIUMPHAL ENTRY (T.E)
3) CURSING OF FIG TREE (C.F)
4) CLEANSING OF TEMPLE (C.T)

GOSPEL OF JOHN: J.A > NEXT DAY T.E   (X C.F)
(JOHN 12)

SYNOPTIC GOSPELS: Matt: T.E > C.T **SAME DAY** > NEXT DAY C.F
(MATT 21, MARK 11, LUKE 19)

Mark: T.E > NEXT DAY C.F > C.T **SAME DAY**

Luke: T.E > C.T **SAME DAY**   (X C.F)

CHAPTER 2

THE FOUR KEY EVENTS IN LINEAR TIME

Now that we know how these four key events flow we can begin to place them in a linear time which should help us see how these events also produce a cycle of events where the ending brings us back to a beginning. This mysterious cycle of these four key events is probably why the earth has a 360 degree circle and why the months of the year prophetically add up to 360 days (12 months of 30 days each), thus helping us to see that God's timing isn't limited to our linear understanding of timing.

So let's begin with placing the day of the Triumphal Entry (T.E), which as we already know happens the day after the anointing of Jesus, which in the gospel of John would place the T.E on the 9th day in the gospel of John but the T.E is on 13th day in the three synoptic gospels.

See the following chart -

THE MYSTERY OF 3 DAYS DIFFERENCE IN THE GOSPELS

GOSPELS FLOW OF KEY EVENTS

1	2	3	4	5	6	7
8 J.A	9 T.E	10	11	12 J.A	13 T.E	14 PASSOVER

GOSPEL OF JOHN: J.A > NEXT DAY T.E (X C.F)
(JOHN 12)

SYNOPTIC GOSPELS: Matt: T.E > C.T SAME DAY > NEXT DAY C.F
(MATT 21, MARK 11, LUKE 19)

Mark: T.E > NEXT DAY C.F > C.T SAME DAY

Luke: T.E > C.T SAME DAY (X C.F)

Once we have placed the second key event (T.E), we can now add the fourth key event- the cleansing of the temple (C.T), because we know it happens on the same day as the triumphal entry in the gospel of John and in two of the three synoptic gospels- the gospel of Matthew and Luke, but remember the cleansing of the temple in the gospel of Mark happens the *day after* the triumphal entry. See next two charts -

THE MYSTERY OF 3 DAYS DIFFERENCE IN THE GOSPELS

GOSPELS FLOW OF KEY EVENTS

1	2	3	4	5	6	7
8 J.A	9 T.E & C.T	10	11	12 J.A	13 T.E & C.T	14 PASSOVER

GOSPEL OF JOHN: J.A > NEXT DAY T.E (X C.F)
(JOHN 12)

SYNOPTIC GOSPELS: Matt: T.E > C.T > NEXT DAY C.F
(MATT 21, MARK 11, LUKE 19)   SAME DAY

Mark: T.E > NEXT DAY C.F > C.T
                     SAME DAY

Luke: T.E > C.T   (X C.F)
      SAME DAY

THE MYSTERY OF 3 DAYS DIFFERENCE IN THE GOSPELS

GOSPELS FLOW OF KEY EVENTS

1	2	3	4	5	6	7
8 J.A	9 T.E & C.T	10	11	12 J.A	13 T.E & CT	14 C.F (MK C.T) PASSOVER

GOSPEL OF JOHN: J.A > NEXT DAY T.E   (X C.F)
(JOHN 12)

SYNOPTIC GOSPELS: Matt: T.E > C.T SAME DAY > NEXT DAY C.F (WITHERED AT ONCE)
(MATT 21, MARK 11, LUKE 19)

Mark: T.E > NEXT DAY C.F > C.T SAME DAY   (IN THE MORNING FIG TREE SEEN WITHERED)

Luke: T.E > C.T SAME DAY   (X C.F)

25

And now the third key event can now be placed, the cursing of the fig tree (C.F)- which isn't mentioned in the gospel of John or Luke, but it is in Matthew and Mark, and it happens in those two gospels on the day after the triumphal entry, being on the same day as the cleansing of the temple in Mark, but the day after the cleansing of the temple in Matthew.

So once, we have these four key events in order we can now place them within the timing of the beginning of time, using the days that are outlined in the first chapter of the gospel of John, which then follows into the cleansing of the temple in chapter 2, which we now know happens on the same day as the triumphal entry and follows after it, thus bringing us back to the beginning, hence the end brings us back to the beginning, with the three-day difference separating them, for a prophetic 'Sign of Jonah' event to happen before the Passion of the Christ even began! See the following chart which shows how the cleansing of the temple happens on the 14th day in the gospel of Mark, before Passover began in the evening of that day, which Jesus did at the temple, while His disciples were making preparations for the Passover in the upper room. Therefore, because we can also see how the gospel of Mark has the cleansing of the temple and the cursing of the fig tree happening *the day after* the triumphal entry, this shows us how time moved ahead in the three synoptic gospels by an extra day for the Passion of the Christ., see the final chart, to see how the night of His betrayal was the 13th night in the gospel of John (i.e. before Passover, John 13:1) but yet it was the 14th night (Passover Night) in the three synoptic gospels.

THE MYSTERY OF 3 DAYS DIFFERENCE IN THE GOSPELS

CLEANSES TEMPLE IN JOHN 2

(NEW MOON DAY) In the beginning... the Word becomes flesh & John the Baptist

NEXT DAY	NEXT DAY	THIRD DAY	4	5	6	7
1 Behold the Lamb of God	**2** Jesus Calls His First Disciples	**3** Wedding at Cana Six big water jars	GOES TO CAPERNAUM AND STAYS THERE FOR A FEW DAYS			
8 J.A	**9** T.E & C.T	**10** THE SIGN OF JONAH	**11** 3 DAYS AND 3 NIGHTS	**12**	**13** T.E & CT	**14** C.F [MK C.T] PASSOVER

THE MYSTERY OF 3 DAYS DIFFERENCE IN THE GOSPELS

CLEANSES TEMPLE IN JOHN 2

(NEW MOON DAY) In the beginning... the Word becomes flesh & John the Baptist

NEXT DAY	NEXT DAY	THIRD DAY	4	5	6	7
1 Behold the Lamb of God	**2** Jesus Calls His First Disciples	**3** Wedding at Cana Six big water Jars	_____ GOES TO CAPERNAUM AND STAYS THERE FOR A FEW DAYS _____			
8 J.A	**9** T.E & C.T	**10**	**11**	**12**	**13** THE NIGHT OF HIS BETRAYAL	**14** JESUS LAMB OF GOD PASSOVER
			12 J.A	**13** T.E & C.T	**14** Mark – C.T & C.F PASSOVER THE NIGHT OF HIS BETRAYAL	**15** JESUS GAVE UP HIS SPIRIT ON CROSS AFTER 3 HRS DARKNESS

The Gospel of Mark reveals that the cleansing of the temple happens the DAY AFTER the other synoptic gospels, hence Gos. of Mark reveals how and when the day moves ahead in the three synoptic gospels, causing the Gos. of John to run a day behind them during the Passion of the Christ.

This also explains why the fig tree withers at once in Matt 21:18-22, but in Mark 11:12-25 it withers in the morning the next day.

This is also revealed in The Dual Passover Night Timeline!

The Gospel of John is running a day behind the three synoptic gospels, therefore Jesus Christ, the Lamb of God, was slain on 14th day before Passover began (6pm) in the Gospel of John, and at that very same moment some of the saints of old were raised- which explains how it was possible for Jesus to say to thief on cross -"Today you will be with me in paradise."

CHAPTER 3

THE FOUR KEY EVENTS IN 2022

So now we have a better understanding of the linear time flow of the key events, we can now use *The Overcomer Calendar* to see how these key events, notably The Triumphal Entry, the Cursing of the Fig Tree and the Cleansing of the Temple, are to happen in our day today, using the Hebrew lunar calendar template (using the full moon as the new moon) and also the Gregorian lunar calendar template (using the dark moon as the new moon).

The scriptural calendar dates for the four key events after the 'Sign of Jonah' (three-day difference) are therefore between 13th -14th days of the first month on the Hebrew Calendar template, bearing in mind that the 14th day of the gospel of John is the 15th day in the three synoptic gospels because the gospel of John is running a day behind the three synoptic gospels (see John 13:1, John 18:28, John 19:14,31). Hence, let's look at The Overcomer Calendar to see what dates the 13th and the 14th days of the first month are, on the Hebrew calendar template ...

The Overcomer Calendar #1

NMD: SUNDAY 17th APRIL 2022

MON	TUES	WEDS	THURS	FRI	SAT	SUN
1	2	3	4	5	6	7
1 18 Apr	2 19 Apr	3 20 Apr	4 21 Apr	5 22 Apr	6 23 Apr	7 24 Apr
8 25 Apr	9 26 Apr	10 27 Apr	11 28 Apr	12 29 Apr	**13** 30 Apr	**14** PASSOVER 1 May
15 1st FoUB 2 May	16 2nd FoUB 3 May	17 3rd FoUB 4 May	18 4th FoUB 5 May	19 5th FoUB 6 May	20 6th FoUB 7 May	21 7th FoUB 8 May
22 9 May	23 10 May	24 11 May	25 12 May	26 13 May	27 14 May	28 15 May
29						

Look at how the key events, which include the Triumphal Entry, that happen between 13th - 14th days of the first month are 30th April - 1st May 2022 which is when the dark moon happens, which could also explain why the soldiers brought torches and lanterns when they arrested Jesus because it confirms it was a dark moon on Passover Night, see John 18:3.

Now let's look at the Gentile lunar calendar for 30th April - 1st May 2022, to show us it's the true day of Pentecost, being the fifth new moon as it uses the dark moon as the new moon...

The OVERCOMER CALENDAR

NMD: SATURDAY 30th APRIL 2022 — #5

SUN	MON	TUES	WEDS	THURS	FRI	SAT
1	2	3	4	5	6	7
1 (1 May)	2	3	4	5	6	7
8	9	10	11	12	13	14
15	16	17	18	19	20	21
22	23	24	25	26	27	28
29						

And if the fifth month begins after the new moon has happened (30th April 20:30 UTC) then it will be 1st May for the New Moon Day of the 5th Month...

The Overcomer Calendar

NMD: SUNDAY 1st MAY 2022 — #5

MON	TUES	WEDS	THURS	FRI	SAT	SUN
1	2	3	4	5	6	7
1 2 May	2	3	4	5	6	7
8	9	10	11	12	13	14
15	16	17	18	19	20	21
22	23	24	25	26	27	28
29						

Therefore, on the Gentile lunar calendar (that uses the dark moon for the new moon), the 30th April - 1st May 2022 is also the 5th dark new moon of 2022, which is the New Moon Day of the fifth month, hence the Day of Pentecost (using a Dual Pentecost Count in Leviticus 23:15-16, not just one count reworded again). So the torches and lanterns that the Gentile soldiers held when they arrested Jesus on the night of Passover on the Hebrew calendar (14th day of 1st month), could also represent the pentecostal fire of the Holy Spirit for the Gentiles as being the day of Pentecost on the new moon day of the fifth month at the same time as Passover for the Jews! Therefore, the 13th-14th days of the first month of the Hebrew calendar template and the fifth new moon of the fifth month on the Gregorian lunar calendar template, both happen between 30th April - 1st May 2022. This time period is so significant in our day because it also includes the other two significant events: the cursing of the fig tree and the cleansing of the temple, which are all connected to the transformation of Christians on the Day of His Visitation (His appearing).

So can you see how significant the 30th - 1st April 2022 truly is for the day of His visitation, at God's appointed time that is not by anyone's own thinking, but by the revelation of the Spirit that comes from the mysteries that are within the scriptures but are kept hidden from the wise and learned and yet revealed to those who ask, seek and knock.

Call unto me, and I will answer thee, and shew thee great and mighty things, which thou knowest not. (Jeremiah 33:3)

So let's now take a quick look at the true scriptural

dual count (two counts) to get to the day of Pentecost for this blessed generation, which is found in *Leviticus 23:15-16 'And ye shall count unto you from the morrow after the sabbath, from the day that ye brought the sheaf of the wave offering; seven sabbaths shall be complete: Even unto the morrow after the seventh sabbath shall ye number fifty days; and ye shall offer a new meat offering unto the LORD.'* There are two counts from both scripture verses, not one count that's been reworded again, that many erroneously teach. The reason why it is two counts is because when you do both counts from the point of the when the count begins (the day of first fruits - which is the resurrection day) then you *always* arrive at the beginning of the fifth month which is a 100th day count (seven weeks of 49 days and then another 50 days to the day it gets to - the 100th day). Therefore the day of Pentecost is found in the fifth month and not in the third month that many believe and have erroneously taught because they believe it's just one count of seven weeks to the day it gets to - 50th day. They also teach that 'pentecost' means 'fifty' but that is again wrong, because the word *'pente'* comes from the Greek and means *'five'*, i.e. Pentagon which is a five sided/angled object from the Greek word 'pentagonos'.

However, because the Gentile calendar starts the new year from January, in comparison to the Hebrew calendar which begins in Springtime, there is also a three month advancement of time - which is one whole season! Therefore, by starting the Pentecost count from the first month of the Gregorian lunar calendar in January (winter) we arrive at the day of Pentecost in springtime, whereas the Hebrew (and even the traditional Christian) calendar would not have Pentecost until later on, because they would only be just starting to count from springtime not ending the count at springtime!

This brings us to the relevance of the third key event, the cursing of the fig tree which explains why Jesus cursed the fig tree just before He went through His passion, *'And seeing a fig tree afar off having leaves, he came, if haply he might find any thing thereon: and when he came to it, he found nothing but leaves; for the time of figs was not yet. And Jesus answered and said unto it, No man eat fruit of thee hereafter for ever. And his disciples heard it.'* (Mark 11:13-14). He cursed the fig tree because He went to it looking for figs (even though it wasn't the season for figs) and found none so He cursed it. He cursed it because the fig tree did not recognise that the season had changed! The fig tree was approached by Jesus (who created it to bear fruit in its appointed season), thus the Master came to creation, which if it was in unity with God's timing not merely earthly timing, should have known the season had come early! It was still springtime and the fig tree went through it's natural course of developing leaves for that appropriate season, but the season had now been divinely changed by being advanced by a whole season (three months) so had it been observant to what the Spirit of God was showing, it should have known the season was now time for figs- even though naturally it wasn't the season for figs!

If the fig tree had been able to recognise the spiritual timing rather than rely on its natural inclination, the fig tree would have been ready with some figs for the Master when He approached it. Therefore, even though it was springtime the fig tree should have adapted accordingly from its natural course to obey God's divine spiritual time and provided figs, even though it wasn't naturally the time for figs; because the divine supreme authority over it was saying it was now the season for figs, and the fig tree (created to be in submission to its Creator) should have obeyed His sovereign will. Hence the time for figs was earlier than it would have been naturally but spiritually it was the right time! Do you think Jesus cursed the fig tree solely because it didn't have figs? No, He cursed it because it didn't recognise the season for bearing figs had advanced from summer into spring, even though naturally it wasn't the season for figs! The fig tree should have allowed itself to be yielded to the Creator's shift of time of the season, rather than remained stubborn in its natural state.

Can you see how this natural fig tree relates to

carnal Christians who refuse to allow themselves to be yielded to spiritual truths and spiritual time, and therefore who continue on in their natural carnal state? Can you see how not being ready for Jesus is because Christians were not able to recognise the spiritual time because they were carnal in their thinking? Can you see how being out of time with God is in contradiction to how we should be walking, that our lives should be yielded completely to His ways through being yielded to the spiritual time, hence His timing? That if we were to allow our minds to be open to spiritual truths we should therefore be able to recognise the spiritual time of God? Of course! So if Jesus cursed the fig tree because it did not recognise the season had spiritually advanced to now be the time to be bearing figs even though naturally it wasn't the season for figs, how do you think it's going to go with Christians when Jesus comes and expects to find fruit in their lives at the appointed time but they weren't ready with any because they carnally and stubbornly thought it's not yet the season for them to do so? Well God says it is! But they have refused to yield to His timing and so they will say to themselves things like "I thought I had more time!!" and "This happened sooner than I was ready for! I thought Pentecost comes in summer, not spring!?!" They thought and thought through their own carnal reasonings, but they didn't yield themselves to be thinking in line with God's thoughts. This is why Jesus will 'cleanse the temple' and bring judgement to the carnal Christians and reward the spiritual obedient Christians who have been living their lives by faith through Christ's life in them, doing the Father's will - they will be transformed and receive the redemption of their bodies, without dying!

Hence, this earlier divinely appointed time for Pentecost is why so many Christians will be taken unawares when this day comes - it will happen when they least expect it, sooner than they thought - just like scripture said it would! This is why Christians should be spiritual, not carnal in their thinking, and therefore spiritual in their living too. As such, the day of Pentecost according to God's divine revelation comes earlier and sooner than most Christians think - in springtime, because God has brought the season forward by starting the Pentecost count in winter, the first month of the Gentile calendar being January 2022, according to a Gentile calendar pattern and yet completing in the first month of the Hebrew calendar template, just before Passover begins on The Overcomer Calendar, as being 30th April - 1st May 2022! Hence, while it began with Passover it ends with Pentecost - but yet it ends before Passover even begins which is why Jesus was put into the tomb before Passover began in the gospel of John 19:31 - a High Sabbath was about to begin which is referring to a feast day sabbath (the 1st Day of the Feast of Unleavened Bread which initiates Passover Night);

the three synoptic gospels however were going into a seventh day sabbath because they are running a day ahead than the gospel of John.

Hence, the Triumphal Entry of Christ happens before Passover Night has even started but yet after the Passion of the Christ has been accomplished, including Him being raised on the third day! Which is why we return to the anointing of Jesus at the very beginning, and explains why Jesus said after Mary anointed Him and the disciples moaned as such a waste that Jesus then said to them, 'Let her alone: against the day of my burying hath she kept this.' (John 12:7). Hence she was showing by her faith, that His death and resurrection had already happened even before it did, and yet it did already happen, which is why Lazarus was already raised from the dead before she even anointed Jesus! Isn't scripture absolutely amazing!

Therefore, in conclusion, the four key events all happened between 13th-14th days of the 1st month on the Hebrew calendar template (30th April -1st May 2022) which is *before Passover*, and yet it is also *after His Passion*, which is why it is also the New Moon Day of the fifth month which is the day of Pentecost for the Gentiles. So it's both to the Jew and to the Gentile - one new man in Christ, a new creation, manifested in Christ, through the redemption of our bodies on 30th April-1st May 2022!! Hence, this amazing circle of time brings us right back to before it all began! It is because of this amazing perfection of God's spiritual timing that means we can have great hope that this is indeed the time for when Christ will appear, through the day of His visitation, on The Triumphal Entry of Christ at the fifth new moon of 30th April-1st May 2022, *before* Passover begins and yet also *after* He has gone through His Passion, where we will receive our greatest hope- the redemption of our bodies through Jesus Christ our Lord! All praise and glory to God!

For all timeline charts and other ministry resources please go to www.theovercomercalendar.com

Printed in Great Britain
by Amazon